State of the Union Addresses

George H.W. Bush

STATE OF THE UNION ADDRESSES

BY

George H.W. Bush

State of the Union Address
George H.W. Bush
January 31, 1990

Tonight, I come not to speak about the "State of the Government", not to detail every new initiative we plan for the coming year, nor describe every line in the budget. I'm here to speak to you and to the American people about the State of the Union about our world, the changes we've seen, the challenges we face. And what that means for America.

There are singular moments in history, dates that divide all that goes before from all that comes after. And many of us in this chamber have lived much of our lives in a world whose fundamental features were defined in 1945. And the events of that year decreed the shape of nations, the pace of progress, freedom or oppression for millions of people around the world.

Nineteen Forty-Five provided the common frame of reference the compass points of the postwar era we've relied upon to understand ourselves. And that was our world until now. The events of the year just ended, the Revolution of '89, have been a chain reaction, changes so striking that it marks the beginning of a new era in the world's affairs.

Think back think back just twelve short months ago to the world we knew as 1989 began.

One year, one year ago the people of Panama lived in fear under the thumb of a dictator. Today democracy is restored. Panama is free.

"Operation Just Cause" has achieved its objective. And the number of military personel in Panama is now very close to what it was before the operation began. And tonight I am announcing that before the end of February the additional numbers of American troops, the brave men and women of our armed forces who made this mission a success, will be back home.

A year ago in Poland, Lech Walesa declared he was ready to open a dialogue with the Communist rulers of that country. And today, with the future of a free Poland in their own hands, members of Solidarity lead the Polish government.

And a year ago, freedom's playwright, Vaclav Havel, languished as a prisoner in Prague. And today it's Vaclav Havel, President of Czechoslovakia.

And one year ago Erich Honecker of East Germany claimed history as his guide. He predicted the Berlin Wall would last another hundred years. And today, less than one year later, it's the wall that's history.

Remarkable events, remarkable events, events that fulfill the long-held hopes of the American people. Events that validate the longstanding goals of American policy, a policy based upon a single shining principle: the cause of freedom.

America, not just the nation, but an idea alive in the minds of the people, everywhere. As this new world takes shape, America stands at the center of a widening circle of freedom, today, tomorrow and into the next century.

Our nation is the enduring dream of every immigrant who ever set foot on these shores, and the millions still struggling to be free. This nation, this idea called America was and always will be a new world, our new world.

At a workers' rally in a place called Branik on the outskirts of Prague the idea called America is alive. A worker, dressed in grimy overalls, rises to speak at the factory gates. And he begins his speech to his fellow citizens with these words, words of a distant revolution: "We hold these truths to be self-evident. That all men are created equal, that they are endowed by their creator with certain unalienable rights, and that among these are life, liberty and the pursuit of happiness." It's no secret here at home freedom's door opened long ago. The cornerstones of this free society have already been set in place: democracy, competition, opportunity, private investment, stewardship, and of course, leadership.

And our challenge today is to take this democratic system of ours, a system second to none, and make it better:

A better America where there's a job for whoever wants one;

Where women working outside the home can be confident their children are in safe and loving care, and where Government works to expand child alternatives for parents.

Where we reconcile the needs of a clean environment and a strong economy.

Where "Made in the USA" is recognized around the world as the symbol of quality and progress,

And where every one of us enjoys the same opportunities to live, to work and to contribute to society. And where, for the first time, the American mainstream includes all of our disabled citizens.

Where everyone has a roof over his head, and where the homeless get the help they need to live in dignity.

Where our schools challenge and support our kids and our teachers, and every one of them makes the grade,

Where every street, every city, every school and every child is drug-free.

And finally, and finally, where no American is forgotten. Our hearts go out to our hostages, our hostages who are ceaselessly in our minds and in our efforts. That's part of the future we want to see, the future we can make for ourselves. But dreams alone won't get us there. We need to extend our horizon, to commit to the long view. And our mission for the future starts today.

In the tough competitive markets around the world, America faces the great challenges and great opportunities. And we know that we can succeed in the global economic arena of the 90's. But to meet that challenge we must make some fundamental changes, some crucial investments in ourselves.

Yes, we are going to invest in America. This Administration is determined to encourage the creation of capital, capital of all kinds. Physical capital: everything from our farms and factories to our workshops and production lines, all that is needed to produce and deliver quality goods and quality services. Intellectual, intellectual capital: the source of ideas that spark tomorrow's products. And of course human capital: the talented work force that we'll need to compete in the global market.

And let me tell you, if we ignore human capital, if we lose the spirit of American ingenuity, the sprit that is the hallmark of the AMERICAN worker, that would be bad. The American worker is the most productive worker in the world.

We need to save more. We need to expand the pool of capital for new investments that mean more jobs and more growth. And that's the idea behind the new initiative I call the Family Savings Plan, which I will send to Congress tomorrow.

We need to cut the tax on capital gains, encourage, encourage risk-takers, especially those in small businesses, to take those steps that translate into economic reward, jobs, and a better life for all of us.

We'll do what it takes to invest in America's future. The budget commitment is there. The money is there. It's there for research and development, R and D, a record high. It's there for our housing initiative, hope, H-O-P-E, to help everyone from first-time homebuyers to the homeless. The money's there to keep our kids drug-free, 70 percent more than when I took office in 1989. It's there for space exploration, and its there for education, another record high.

And one more, and one more thing. Last fall at the education summit, the governors and I agreed to look for ways to help make sure that our kids are ready to learn the very first day they walk into the classroom. And I've made good on that commitment by proposing a record increase in funds, an extra half billion dollars, for something near and dear to all of us: Head Start.

Education is the one investment that means more for our future, because it means the most for our children. Real improvement in our schools is not simply a matter of spending more. It's a matter of asking more, expecting more, of our schools, our teachers, of our kids, of our parents and of ourselves. And that's why tonight, and that's why tonight, I am announcing America's education goals, goals developed with enormous cooperation from the nation's governors. And if I might I'd like to say I'm very pleased that Governor Gardner and Governor Clinton, Governor Branstad, Governor Campbell, all of whom were very key in these discussion, these deliberations, are with us here tonight.

By the, by the year 2000, every child must start school ready to learn. The United States must increase the high school graduation rate to no less than 90 percent. And we are going to make sure our schools' diplomas mean something. In critical subjects, at the fourth, eighth, and 12th grades, we must assess our students' performance.

By the, by the year 2000 U.S. students must be the first in the world in math and science achievement. Every American adult must be a skilled, literate worker and citizen. Every school must offer the kind of disciplined environment that makes it possible for our kids to learn. And every school in America must be drug-free.

Ambitious aims? Of course. Easy to do? Far from it. But the future's at stake. The nation will not accept anything less than excellence in education.

These investments will help keep America competitive. And I know this about the American people: we welcome competition. We'll match our ingenuity, our energy, our experience, and technology our spirit and enterprise against anyone. But let the competition be free, but let it also be fair. America is ready.

Since we really mean it, and since we're serious about being ready to meet our challenge, we're getting our own house in order. We have made real progress. Seven years ago, the Federal deficit was 6 percent of our gross national product, 6 percent. In the new budget I sent up two days ago the deficit is down to 1 percent of GNP.

That budget brings Federal spending under control. It meets the Gramm-Rudman target. It brings the deficit down further. And balances the budget by 1993, with no new taxes.

And let me tell you, there's still more than enough Federal spending. For most of us, $1.2 trillion is still a lot of money.

And once the budget is balanced, we can operate the way every family must when it has bills to pay. We won't leave it to our children and grandchildren. Once it's balanced, we will start paying off the national debt.

And there's something more, and there's something more we owe the generations of the future: stewardship, the safekeeping of America's precious environmental inheritance.

As just one sign of how serious we are, we will elevate the Environmental Protection Agency to Cabinet rank. Not, not more bureaucracy, not more red tape, but the certainty that here at home, and especially in our dealings with other nations, environmental issues have the status they deserve.

This year's budget provides over $2 billion in new spending to protect our environment, with over $1 billion for global change research, and a new initiative I call America the Beautiful to expand our national parks and wildlife preserves and improve recreational facilities on public lands.

And something else, something that will help keep this country clean, from our forest land to the inner cities, and keep America beautiful for generations to come, the money to plant a billion trees a year.

And tonight, and tonight let me say again to all the members of the Congress, the American people did not send us here to bicker. There is work to do, and they sent us here to get it done. And once again, in the spirit of cooperation I offer my hand to all of you. And let's work together to do the will of the people--clean air, child care, the educational excellence act, crime and drugs. It's time to act. The farm bill, transportation policy, product liability reform, enterprise zones. It's time to act together.

And there's one thing I hope we can agree on. It's about our commitments. And I'm talking about Social Security.

To every American out there on Social Security, to every, every American supporting that system today, and to everyone counting on it when they retire, we made a promise to you, and we are going to keep it.

We, we rescued the system in 1983 and it's sound again, bipartisan arrangement. Our budget fully funds today's benefits and it assures that future benefits will be funded as well. And the last thing we need to do is mess around with Social Security.

There's one more problem we need to address. We must give careful consideration to the recommendations of the health care studies under way now. And that's why tonight, I am asking Dr. Sullivan, Lou Sullivan, Secretary of Health and Human Services, to lead a Domestic Policy Council review of recommendations on the quality, accessibility and cost of our nation's health care system. I am committed to bring the staggering costs of health care under control.

The State of the Government does indeed depend on many of us in this very chamber. But the State of the Union depends on all Americans. We must maintain the democratic decency that makes a nation out of millions of individuals. And I've been appalled at the recent mail bombings across this country. Every one of us must confront and condemn racism, anti-Semitism, bigotry and hate. Not next week, not tomorrow, but right now. Every single one of us.

The State of the Union depends on whether we help our neighbor, claim the problems of our community as our own. We've got to step forward when there's trouble, lend a hand, be what I call a point of light to a stranger in need. We've got to take the time after a busy day to sit down and read with our kids, help them with their homework, pass along the values we had as children. And that's how we sustain the State of the Union.

Every effort is important. It all adds up. It's doing the things that give democracy meaning. It all adds up to who we are and who we will be.

And let me say, that so long as we remember the American idea, so long as we live up to the American ideal, the State of the Union will remain sound and strong.

And to those who worry that we've lost our way, well, I want you to listen to parts of a letter written by James Markwell, Pvt. 1st Class James Markwell, a 20-year-old Army medic to the First Battalion, 75th Rangers. It's dated Dec. 18, the day before our armed forces went into action in Panama. It's a letter servicemen write--and hope will never, ever be sent. And sadly, Private Markwell's mother did receive this letter. She passed it on to me out there in Cincinnati.

And here is some of what he wrote: "I've never been afraid of death, but I know he is waiting at the corner...I've been trained to kill and to save, and so has everyone else. I am frightened of what lays beyond the fog, and yet... do not mourn for me. Revel in the life that I have died to give you... But most of all, don't forget that the Army was my choice. Something that I wanted to do. Remember I joined the Army to serve my country and inure that you are free to do what you want and to live your lives freely."

Let me add that Private Markwell was among the first to see battle in Panama, and among the first to fall. But he knew what he believed in. He carried the idea we call America in his heart.

I began tonight speaking about the changes we've seen this past year. There is a new world of challenges and opportunities before us. And there is a need for leadership that only America can provide.

Nearly 40 years ago, in his last address to the Congress, President Harry Truman predicted such a time would come. He said, "As our world grows stronger, more united, more attractive to men on both sides of the Iron Curtain, then inevitably there will come a time of change within the Communist world." Today, that change is taking place.

For more than 40 years, America and its allies held Communism in check and insured that democracy would continue to exist. And today, with Communism crumbling, our aim must be to insure democracy's advance, to take the lead in forging peace and freedom's best hope, a great and growing commonwealth of free nations.

And to the Congress and to all Americans, I say it is time to acclaim a new consensus at home and abroad, a common vision of the peaceful world we want to see.

Here in our own hemisphere it is time for all the people of the Americas, North and South, to live in freedom.

In the Far East and Africa, it's time for the full flowering of free governments and free markets that have served the engine of progress.

It is time to offer our hand to the emerging democracies of Eastern Europe so that continent, for too long a continent divided, can see a future whole and free.

It's time to build on our new relationship with the Soviet Union, to endorse and encourage a peaceful process of internal change toward democracy and economic opportunity.

We are in a period of great transition, great hope, and yet great uncertainty. We recognize that the Soviet military threat in Europe is diminishing, but we see little change in Soviet strategic modernization. And, therefore, we must sustain our own strategic offense modernization and the Strategic Defense Initiative.

But the time is right to move forward on a conventional arms control agreement to move us to more appropriate levels of military forces in Europe, a coherent defense program that insures the U.S. will continue to be a catalyst for peaceful change in Europe. And I've consulted with leaders of NATO. In fact I spoke by phone with President Gorbachev just today.

And I agree with our European allies that an American military presence in Europe is essential and that it should not be solely tied to the Soviet military presence in Eastern Europe.

But our troop levels can still be lower. And so tonight I am announcing a major new step for a further reduction in U.S. and Soviet manpower in Central and Eastern Europe to 195,000 on each side.

This number, this number, this level, reflects the advice of our senior military advisers. It's designed to protect American and European interests and sustain NATO's defense strategy. A swift conclusion to our arms control talks--conventional, chemical and strategic--must now be our goal. And that time has come.

Still, we must recognize an unfortunate fact: in many regions of the world tonight the reality is conflict, not peace. Enduring animosities and opposing interests remain. And thus the cause of peace must be served by an America strong enough and sure enough to defend our interests and our ideals. It's this American idea that for the past four decades helped inspire the Revolution of '89.

And here at home, and in the world, there is history in the making, and history to be made. Six months ago, early in this season of change, I stood at the gates of the Gdansk shipyard in Poland at the monument to the fallen workers of Solidarity. It's a monument of simple majesty. Three tall crosses rise up from the stones, and atop each cross, an anchor, an ancient symbol of hope.

The anchor in our world today is freedom. Holding us steady in times of change, a symbol of hope to all the world. And freedom is at the very heart of the idea that is America. Giving life to the idea depends on every one of us. Our anchor has always been faith and family.

In the last few days of this past monumentous year, our family was blessed once more, celebrating the joy of life when a little boy became our 12th grandchild. When I held the little guy for the first time, the troubles at home and abroad seemed manageable, and totally in perspective.

And now I know, I know you're probably thinking, Well, that's just a grandfather talking.

Well, maybe you're right. But I've met a lot of children this past year across this country, as all of you have. Everywhere from the Far East to Eastern Europe. All kids are unique. Yet, all kids are alike. The budding young environmentalist I met this month, who joined me in exploring the Florida Everglades. The Little Leaguers I played catch with in Poland, ready to go from Warsaw to the World Series. And even the kids who are ill or alone--and God bless those boarder babies, born addicted to drugs and AIDS--coping with problems no child should have to face. But, you know, when it comes to hope and the future, every kid is the same: full of dreams, ready to take on the world, all special because they are the very future of freedom. And to them belongs this new world I've been speaking about.

And so tonight, I'm going to ask something of every one of you. Now let me start with my generation, with the grandparents out there. You are our living link with the past. Tell your grandchildren the story of struggles waged at home and abroad, of sacrifices freely made for freedom's sake. And tell them your own story as well, because every American has a story to tell.

And parents, your children look to you for direction and guidance. Tell them of faith and family. Tell them we are one nation under God. Teach them that of all the many gifts they can receive, liberty is their most precious legacy. And of all the gifts they can give, the greatest, the greatest is helping others.

And to the children and young people out there tonight, with you rests our hope, all that America will mean in the years and decades ahead. Fix your vision on a new century, your century, on dreams we cannot see, on the destiny that is yours and yours alone.

And finally, let all Americans, all of us here in this chamber, the symbolic center of democracy, affirm our allegiance to this idea we call America. And let us remember that the State of the Union depends upon each and every one of us.

God bless all of you. And may God bless this great nation, the United States of America.

State of the Union Address
George H.W. Bush
January 29, 1991

Mr. President, Mr. Speaker, members of the United States Congress.

I come to this house of the people to speak to you and all Americans, certain we stand at a defining hour.

Halfway around the world, we are engaged in a great struggle in the skies and on the seas and sands. We know why we're there. We are Americans--part of something larger than ourselves.

For two centuries we've done the hard work of freedom. And tonight we lead the world in facing down a threat to decency and humanity.

What is at stake is more than one small country, it is a big idea--a new world order, where diverse nations are drawn together in common cause to achieve the universal aspirations of mankind: peace and security, freedom, and the rule of law. Such is a world worthy of our struggle, and worthy of our children's future.

The community of nations has resolutely gathered to condemn and repel lawless aggression. Saddam Hussein's unprovoked invasion--his ruthless, systematic rape of a peaceful neighbor--violated everything the community of nations holds dear. The world has said this aggression would not stand, and it will not stand.

Together, we have resisted the trap of appeasement, cynicism and isolation that gives temptation to tyrants. The world has answered Saddam's invasion with 12 United Nations resolutions, starting with a demand for Iraq's immediate and unconditional withdrawal, and backed up by forces from 28 countries of six continents. With few exceptions, the world now stands as one.

The end of the cold war has been a victory for all humanity. A year and a half ago, in Germany, I said our goal was a Europe whole and free. Tonight, Germany is united. Europe has become whole and free, and America's leadership was instrumental in making it possible.

The principle that has guided us is simple: our objective is to help the Baltic peoples achieve their aspirations, not to punish the Soviet Union. In our recent discussions with the Soviet leadership we have been given representations, which, if fulfilled, would result in the withdrawal of some Soviet forces, a re-opening of dialogue with the republics, and a move away from violence.

We will watch carefully as the situation develops. And we will maintain our contact with the Soviet leadership to encourage continued commitment to democratization and reform.

If it is possible, I want to continue to build a lasting basis for U.S.-Soviet cooperation, for a more peaceful future for all mankind.

The triumph of democratic ideas in Eastern Europe and Latin America, and the continuing struggle for freedom elsewhere around the world all confirm the wisdom of our nation's founders.

Tonight, we work to achieve another victory, a victory over tyranny and savage aggression.

We in this Union enter the last decade of the 20th Century thankful for all our blessings, steadfast in our purpose, aware of our difficulties and responsive to our duties at home and around the world.

For two centuries, America has served the world as an inspiring example of freedom and democracy. For generations, America has led the struggle to preserve and extend the blessings of liberty. And today, in a rapidly changing world, American leadership is indispensable. Americans know that leadership brings burdens, and requires sacrifice.

But we also know why the hopes of humanity turn to us. We are Americans; we have a unique responsibility to do the hard work of freedom. And when we do, freedom works.

The conviction and courage we see in the Persian Gulf today is simply the American character in action. The indomitable spirit that is contributing to this victory for world peace and justice is the same spirit that gives us the power and the potential to meet our challenges at home.

We are resolute and resourceful. If we can selflessly confront evil for the sake of good in a land so far away, then surely we can make this land all it should be.

If anyone tells you America's best days are behind her, they're looking the wrong way.

Tonight, I come before this house, and the American people, with an appeal for renewal. This is not merely a call for new government initiatives, it is a call for new initiative in government, in our communities, and from every American--to prepare for the next American century.

America has always led by example. So who among us will set this example? Which of our citizens will lead us in this next American century? Everyone who steps forward today, to get one addict off drugs; to convince one troubled teen-ager not to give up on life; to comfort one AIDS patient; to help one hungry child.

We have within our reach the promise of renewed America. We

can find meaning and reward by serving some purpose higher than our-selves--a shining purpose, the illumination of a thousand points of light. It is expressed by all who know the irresistible force of a child's hand, of a friend who stands by you and stays there--a volunteer's generous gesture, an idea that is simply right.

The problems before us may be different, but the key to solving them remains the same: it is the individual--the individual who steps forward. And the state of our Union is the union of each of us, one to the other: the sum of our friendships, marriages, families and communi-ties.

We all have something to give. So if you know how to read, find someone who can't. If you've got a hammer, find a nail. If you're not hungry, not lonely, not in trouble--seek out someone who is.

Join the community of conscience. Do the hard work of freedom. That will define the state of our Union.

Since the birth of our nation, "we the people" has been the source of our strength. What government can do alone is limited, but the po-tential of the American people knows no limits.

We are a nation of rock-solid realism and clear-eyed idealism. We are Americans. We are the nation that believes in the future. We are the nation that can shape the future.

And we've begun to do just that, by strengthening the power and choice of individuals and families.

Together, these last two years, we've put dollars for child care di-rectly in the hands of patients instead of bureaucracies, unshackled the potential of Americans with disabilities, applied the creativity of the marketplace in the service of the environment, for clean air, and made homeownership possible for more Americans.

The strength of a democracy is not in bureaucracy, it is in the people and their communities. In everything we do, let us unleash the potential of our most precious resource--our citizens. We must return to families, communities, counties, cities, states and institutions of every kind, the power to chart their own destiny, and the freedom and opportunity provided by strong economic growth. That's what America is all about.

I know, tonight, in some regions of our country, people are in genuine economic distress. I hear them.

Earlier this month Kathy Blackwell of Massachusetts wrote me about what can happen when the economy slows down, saying, "My heart is aching, and I think that you should know--your people out here are hurting badly."

I understand. And I'm not unrealistic about the future. But there are reasons to be optimistic about our economy.

First, we don't have to fight double-digit inflation. Second, most industries won't have to make big cuts in production because they don't have big inventories piled up. And third, our exports are running solid and strong. In fact, American businesses are exporting at a record rate.

So let's put these times in perspective. Together, since 1981, we've created almost 20 million jobs, cut inflation in half and cut interest rates in half.

Yes, the largest peacetime economic expansion in history has been temporarily interrupted. But our economy is still over twice as large as our closest competitor.

We will get this recession behind us and return to growth soon. We will get on our way to a new record of expansion, and achieve the competitive strength that will carry us into the next American century.

We should focus our efforts today on encouraging economic growth, investing in the future and giving power and opportunity to the individual.

We must begin with control of Federal spending. That's why I'm submitting a budget that holds the growth in spending to less than the rate of inflation. And that's why, amid all the sound and fury of last year's budget debate, we put into law new, enforceable spending caps so that future spending debates will mean a battle of ideas, not a bidding war.

Though controversial, the budget agreement finally put the Federal Government on a pay-as-you-go basis, and cut the growth of debt by nearly $500 billion. And that frees funds for saving and job-creating investment.

Now, let's do more. My budget again includes tax-free family savings accounts; penalty-free withdrawals from I. R. A.'s for first-time homebuyers; and, to increase jobs and growth, a reduced tax for long-term capital gains.

I know their are differences among us about the impact and the effects of a capital gains incentive. So tonight I am asking the Congressional leaders and the Federal Reserve to cooperate with us in a study, led by Chairman Alan Greenspan, to sort out our technical differences so that we can avoid a return to unproductive partisan bickering.

But just as our efforts will bring economic growth now and in the future, they must also be matched by long-term investments for the next American century.

That requires a forward-looking plan of action, and that's exactly what we will be sending to the Congress. We have prepared a detailed series of proposals, that include: A budget that promotes investment in America's future--in children, education, infrastructure, space and high technology. Legislation to achieve excellence in education, building on the partnership forged with the 50 governors at the education summit, enabling parents to choose their children's schools and helping to make America No. 1 in math and science. A blueprint for a new national highway system, a critical investment in our transportation infrastructure. A research and development agenda that includes record levels of Federal investment and a permanent tax credit to strengthen private R and D and create jobs. A comprehensive national energy strategy that calls for energy conservation and efficiency, increased development and greater use of alternative fuels. A banking reform plan to bring America's financial system into the 21st Century, so that our banks remain safe and secure and can continue to make job-creating loans for our factories, businesses, and homebuyers. I do think there has been too much pessimism. Sound banks should be making more sound loans, now. And interest rates should be lower, now. In addition to these proposals, we must recognize that our economic strength depends upon being competitive in world markets. We must continue to expand America's exports. A successful Uruguay Round of world trade negotiations will create more real jobs, and more real growth, for all nations. You and I know that if the playing field is level, America's workers and farmers can outwork and outproduce anyone, anytime, anywhere.

And with the Mexican free trade agreement and our Enterprise for the Americas Initiative we can help our partners strengthen their economies and move toward a free trade zone throughout this entire hemisphere.

The budget also includes a plan of action right here at home to put more power and opportunity in the hands of the individual. That means new incentives to create jobs in our inner cities by encouraging investment through enterprise zones. It also means tenant control and ownership of public housing. Freedom and the power to choose should not be the privilege of wealth. They are the birthright of every American.

Civil rights are also crucial to protecting equal opportunity. Every one of us has a responsibility to speak out against racism, bigotry, and hate. We will continue our vigorous enforcement of existing statutes, and I will once again press the Congress to strengthen the laws against employment discrimination without resorting to the use of unfair preferences.

We're determined to protect another fundamental civil right: freedom from crime and the fear that stalks our cities. The Attorney General will soon convene a crime summit of the nation's law-enforcement officials. And to help us support them we need a tough crime control legislation, and we need it now.

As we fight crime, we will fully implement our nation strategy for combatting drug abuse. Recent data show we are making progress, but much remains to be done. We will not rest until the day of the dealer is over, forever.

Good health care is every American's right and every American's responsibility. So we are proposing an aggression program of new prevention initiatives--for infants, for children, for adults, and for the elderly-- to promote a healthier America and to help keep costs from spiraling.

It's time to give people more choice in government by reviving the ideal of the citizen politician who comes not to stay, but to serve. One of the reasons there is so much support for term limitations is that the American people are increasingly concerned about big-money influence in politics. We must look beyond the next election, to the next generation. The time has come to put the national interest ahead of the special interest--and totally eliminate political action committees.

That would truly put more competition in elections and more power in the hands of individuals. And where power cannot be put directly into the hands of the individual, it should be moved closer to the people--away from Washington.

The federal government too often treats government programs as if they are of Washington, by Washington, and for Washington. Once established, federal programs seem to become immortal.

It's time for a more dynamic program life cycle. Some programs should increase. Some should decrease. Some should be terminated. And some should be consolidated and turned over to the states.

My budget includes a list of programs for potential turnover totaling more than $20 billion. Working with Congress and the governors, I propose we select at least $15 billion in such programs and turn them over to the states in a single consolidated grant, fully funded, for flexible management by the states.

The value of this turnover approach is straightforward. It allows the Federal Government to reduce overhead. It allows states to manage more flexibly and more efficiently. It moves power and decision-making closer to the people. And it re-enforces a theme of this Administration: appreciation and encouragement of the innovative power of "states as laboratories."

This nation was founded by leaders who understood that power belongs in the hands of the people. They planned for the future. And so must we--here and around the world.

As Americans, we know there are times when we must step forward and accept our responsibility to lead the world away from the dark chaos of dictators, toward the bright promise of a better day.

Almost 50 years ago, we began a long struggle against aggressive totalitarianism. Now we face another defining hour for America and the world.

There is no one more devoted, more committed to the hard work of freedom, than every soldier and sailor, every marine, airman and coast-guardsman-- every man and every woman now serving in the Persian Gulf.

Each of them has volunteered to provide for this nation's defense. And now they bravely struggle to earn for America and for the world and for future generations, a just and lasting peace.

Our commitment to them must be equal of their commitment to our country. They are truly America's finest.

The war in the gulf is not a war we wanted. We worked hard to avoid war. For more than five months we, along with the Arab League, the European Community and the United Nations, tried every diplomatic avenue. U.N. Secretary General Perez de Cuellar; Presidents Gorbachev, Mitterand, Ozal, Mubarak, and Bendjedid; Kings Fahd and Hassan; Prime Ministers Major and Andreotti--just to name a few--all worked for a solution. But time and again Saddam Hussein flatly rejected the path of diplomacy and peace.

The world well knows how this conflict began, and when: it began on August 2nd, when Saddam invaded and sacked a small, defenseless neighbor. And I am certain of how it will end. So that peace can prevail, we will prevail.

Tonight I'm pleased to report that we are on course. Iraq's capacity to sustain war is being destroyed. Our investment, our training, our planning --all are paying off. Time will not be Saddam's salvation.

Our purpose in the Persian Gulf remains constant: to drive Iraq out from Kuwait, to restore Kuwait's legitimate government, and to insure the stability and security of this critical region.

Let me make clear what I mean by the region's stability and security. We do not seek the destruction of Iraq, its culture or its people. Rather, we seek an Iraq that uses its great resources not to destroy, not to serve the ambitions of a tyrant, but to build a better life for itself and its neighbors. We seek a Persian Gulf where conflict is no longer the rule, where the strong are neither tempted nor able to intimidate the weak.

Most Americans know instinctively why we are in the Gulf. They know we had to stop Saddam now, not later. They know this brutal dictator will do anything, will use any weapon, will commit any outrage, no matter how many innocents must suffer.

They know we must make sure that control of the world's oil resources does not fall into his hands only to finance further aggression. They know that we need to build a new, enduring peace--based not on arms races and confrontation, but on shared principles and the rule of law.

And we all realize that our responsibility to be the catalyst for peace in the region does not end with the successful conclusion of this war.

Democracy brings the undeniable value of thoughtful dissent, and we have heard some dissenting voices here at home, some reckless, most responsible. But the fact the all the voices have the right to speak out is one of the reasons we've been united in principle and purpose for 200 years.

Our progress in this great struggle is the result of years of vigilance and a steadfast commitment to a strong defense. Now, with remarkable technological advances like the Patriot missile, we can defend the ballistic missile attacks aimed at innocent civilians.

Looking forward, I have directed that the S.D.I. program be refocused on providing protection from limited ballistic missile strikes, whatever their source. Let us pursue an S.D.I. program that can deal with any future threat to the United States, to our forces overseas and to our friends and allies.

The quality of American technology, thanks to the American worker, has enabled us to successfully deal with difficult military conditions, and help minimize the loss of life. We have given our men and women the very best. And they deserve it.

We all have a special place in our hearts for the families of men and women serving in the Gulf. They are represented here tonight, by Mrs. Norman Schwarzkopf, and to all those serving with him. And to the families, let me say, our forces in the gulf will not stay there one day longer than is necessary to complete their mission.

The courage and success of the R.A.F. pilots--of the Kuwaiti, Saudi, French, Canadians, Italians, the pilots of Qatar and Bahrain--all are proof that for the first time since World War II, the international community is united. The leadership of the United Nations, once only a hoped-for ideal, is now confirming its founders' vision.

I am heartened that we are not being asked to bear alone the financial burden of this struggle. Last year, our friends and allies provided the bulk of the economic costs of Desert Shield, and having now received commitments of over $40 billion for the first three months of 1991, I am confident they will do no less as we move through Desert Storm.

But the world has to wonder what the dictator of Iraq is thinking. If he thinks that by targeting innocent civilians in Israel and Saudi Arabia, that he will gain an advantage--he is dead wrong. If he thinks that he will advance his cause through tragic and despicable environmental terrorism--he is dead wrong. And if he thinks that by abusing coalition P.O.W.s, he will benefit--he is dead wrong.

We will succeed in the Gulf. And when we do, the world community will have sent an enduring warning to any dictator or despot, present or future, who contemplates outlaw aggression.

The world can therefore seize this opportunity to fulfill the long-held promise of a new world order--where brutality will go unrewarded, and aggression will meet collective resistance.

Yes, the United States bears a major share of leadership in this effort. Among the nations of the world, only the United States of America has had both the moral standing, and the means to back it up. We are the only nation on this earth that could assemble the forces of peace.

This is the burden of leadership--and the strength that has made America the beacon of freedom in a searching world.

This nation has never found glory in war. Our people have never wanted to abandon the blessings of home and work, for distant lands and deadly conflict. If we fight in anger, it is only because we have to fight at all. And all of us yearn for a world where we will never have to fight again.

Each of us will measure, within ourselves, the value of this great struggle. Any cost in lives is beyond our power to measure. But the cost of closing our eyes to aggression is beyond mankind's power to imagine.

This we do know: Our cause is just. Our cause is moral. Our cause is right.

Let future generations understand the burden and the blessings of freedom. Let them say, we stood where duty required us to stand.

Let them know that together, we affirmed America, and the world, as a community of conscience.

The winds of change are with us now. The forces of freedom are united. We move toward the next century, more confident than ever, that we have the will at home and abroad, to do what must be done--the hard work of freedom.

May God bless the United States of America.

State of the Union Address
George H.W. Bush
January 28, 1992

Mr. Speaker, Mr. President, distinguished members of Congress, honored guests and fellow citizens:

I mean to speak tonight of big things, of big changes and the promises they hold and of some big problems and how together we can solve them and move our country forward as the undisputed leader of the age.

We gather tonight at a dramatic and deeply promising time in our history, and in the history of man on earth. For in the past 12 months, the world has known changes of almost biblical proportions. And even now, months after the failed coup that doomed a failed system, I am not sure we have absorbed the full impact, the full import of what happened.

But Communism died this year. Even as President, with the most fascinating possible vantage point, there were times when I was so busy helping to manage progress and lead change that I didn't always show the joy that was in my heart But the biggest thing that has happened in the world in my life, in our lives, is this: By the grace of God, America won the Cold War. And there's another to be singled out, though it may seem inelegant. I mean a mass of people called the American taxpayer. No ever thinks to thank the people who pay country's bill or an alliance's bill. But for a half Century now, the American people have shouldered the burden and paid taxes that were higher than they would have been to support a defense that was bigger than it would have been if imperial communism had never existed. But it did. But it doesn't anymore. And here is a fact I wouldn't mind the world acknowledging: The American taxpayer bore the brunt of the burden, and deserves a hunk of the glory.

And so, now, for the first time in 35 years, our strategic bombers stand down. No longer are they on round-the-clock alert. Tomorrow our children will go to school and study history and how plants grow. And they won't have, as my children did, air-raid drills in which they crawl under their desks and cover their heads in case of nuclear war. My grandchildren don't have to do that, and won't have the bad dreams children once had in decades past. There are still threats. But the long drawn-out dread is over.

A year ago tonight I spoke to you at a moment of high peril. American forces had just unleashed Operation Desert Storm. And after 40 days in the desert skies and 4 days on the ground, the men and women of America's armed forces and our allies accomplished the goals that I declared, and that you endorsed: we liberated Kuwait.

Soon after, the Arab world and Israel sat down to talk seriously, and comprehensively, about peace, an historic first. And soon after that, at Christmas, the last American hostages came home. Our policies were vindicated.

Much good can come from the prudent use of power. And much good can come from this: A world once divided into two armed camps now recognizes one sole and pre-eminent power, the United States of America. And this they regard with no dread. For the world trusts us with power, and the world is right. They trust us to be fair, and restrained. They trust us to be on the side of decency. They trust us to do what's right.

I use those words advisedly. A few days after the war began, I received a telegram from Joanne Speicher, the wife of the first pilot killed in the gulf, Lieutenant Commander Scott Speicher. Even in her grief, she wanted me to know that some day, when her children were old enough, she would tell them "that their father went away to war because it was the right thing to do". She said it all. It was the right thing to do.

And we did it together. There were honest differences here, in this chamber. But when the war began, you put your partisanship aside and supported our troops. This is still a time for pride, but this is no time to boast. For problems face us, and we must stand together once again and solve them--and not let our country down.

Two years ago, I began planning cuts in military spending that reflected the changes of the new era. But now, this year, with Imperial Communism gone, that process can be accelerated. Tonight I can tell you of dramatic changes in our strategic nuclear force. These are actions we are taking on our own, because they are the right thing to do.

After completing 20 planes for which we have begun procurement, we will shut down production of the B-2 bomber. We will cancel the ICBM program. We will cease production of new warheads for our sea-based missiles. We will stop all production of the peacekeeper missile. And we will not purchase any more advanced cruise missiles.

This weekend I will meet at Camp David with Boris Yeltsin of the Russian Federation. I have informed President Yeltsin that if the commonwealth, the former Soviet Union, will eliminate all land-based multiple-warhead ballistic missiles, I will do the following: We will eliminate all Peacekeeper missiles. We will reduce the number of warheads on Minuteman missiles to one and reduce the number of warheads on our sea-based missiles by about one-third. And we will convert a substantial portion of our strategic to primarily conventional use.

President Yeltsin's early response has been very positive, and I expect our talks at Camp David to be fruitful. I want you to know that for half a century, American presidents have longed to make such decisions and say such words. But even in the midst of celebration, we must keep caution as a friend. For the world is still a dangerous place. Only the dead have seen the end of conflict. And though yesterday's challenges are behind us, tomorrow's are being born.

The Secretary of defense recommended these cuts after consultation with the joint chiefs of staff. And I make them with confidence. But do not misunderstand me: The reductions I have approved will save us an additional $50 billion over the next five years. By 1997 we will have cut defense by 30 percent since I took office. These cuts are deep, and you must know my resolve: this deep, and no deeper. To do less would be insensible to progress, but to do more would be ignorant of history. We must not go back to the days of "the hollow army". We cannot repeat the mistakes made twice in this century when armistice was followed by recklessness and defense was purged as if the world was permanently safe.

I remind you this evening that I have asked for your support in funding a program to protect our country from limited nuclear missile attack. We must have this protection because too many people in too many countries have access to nuclear arms. There are those who say that now we can turn away from the world, that we have no special role, no special place. But we are the United States of America, the leader of the West that has become the leader of the world.

As long as I am President we will continue to lead in support of freedom everywhere, not out of arrogance and not out of altruism, but for the safety and security of our children. This is a fact: Strength in the pursuit of peace is no vice; isolationism in the pursuit of security is no virtue.

Now to our troubles at home. They are not all economic, but the primary problem is our economy. There are some good signs. Inflation, that thief, is down, and interest rates are down. But unemployment is too high, some industries are in trouble and growth is not what it should be. Let me tell you right from the start and right from the heart: I know we're in hard times, but I know something else: This will not stand.

My friends in this chamber, we can bring the same courage and sense of common purpose to the economy that we brought to Desert Storm. And we can defeat hard times together. I believe you will help. One reason is that you're patriots, and you want the best for your country. And I believe that in your hearts you want to put partisanship aside and get the job done, because it's the right thing to do.

The power of America rests in a stirring but simple idea: that people will do great things if only you set them free. Well, we're going to have to set the economy free, for if this age of miracles and wonders has taught us anything, it's that if we can change the world, we can change America.

We must encourage investment. We must make it easier for people to invest money and make new products, new industries, and new jobs. We must clear away obstacles to new growth: high taxes, high regulation, red tape, and yes, wasteful government spending. None of this will happen with a snap of the fingers, but it will happen. And the test of a plan isn't whether it's called new or dazzling. The American people aren't impressed by gimmicks. They're smarter on this score than all of us in this room. The only test of a plan is, It is sound and will it work? We must have a short-term plan to address our immediate needs and heat up the economy. And then we need a long-term plan to keep the combustion going and to guarantee our place in the world economy.

There are certain things that a president can do without Congress, and I am going to do them. I have this evening asked major cabinet departments and federal agencies to institute a 90-day moratorium on any new federal regulations that could hinder growth. In those 90 days, major departments and agencies will carry out a top-to-bottom review of all regulations, old and new, to stop the ones that will hurt growth and speed up those that will help growth.

Further, for the untold number of hard-working, responsible American workers and businessmen and women who've been forced to go without needed bank loans, the banking credit crunch must end. I won't neglect my responsibility for sound regulations that serve the public good, but regulatory overkill must be stopped. And I have instructed our government regulators to stop it.

I have directed Cabinet departments and federal agencies to speed up pro-growth expenditures as quickly as possible. This should put an extra $10 billion into the economy in the next six months. And our new transportation bill provides more than $150 billion for construction and maintenance projects that are vital to our growth and well-being. That means jobs building roads, jobs building bridges and jobs building railways. And I have this evening directed the secretary of the Treasury to change the federal tax withholding tables. With this change, millions of Americans from whom the government withholds more than necessary can now choose to have the government withhold less from their paychecks. Something tells me a number of taxpayers may take us up on this one. This initiative could return about $25 billion back into the economy over the next 12 months, money people can use to help pay for clothing, college or a new car. And finally, working with the Federal Reserve, we will continue to support monetary policy that keeps both interest rates and inflation down.

Now these are the things that I can do. And now, members of Congress, let me tell you what you can do for your country. You must, you must pass the other elements of my plan to meet our economic needs. Everyone knows investment speeds recovery. And I am proposing this evening a change in the alternative minimum tax, and the creation of a new 15% investment tax allowance. This will encourage businesses to accelerate investment and bring people back to work. Real estate has led our economy out of almost all the tough times we've ever had. Once building starts, carpenters and plumbers work, people buy homes and take out mortgages.

My plan would modify the passive-loss rule for active real-estate developers. And it would make it easier for pension plans to purchase real estate. For those Americans who dream of buying a first home but who can't quite afford it, my plan would allow first-time home buyers to withdraw savings from IRAs without penalty and provide a $5000 tax credit for the first purchase of that home.

And finally, my immediate plan calls on Congress to give crucial help to people who own a home, to every one who has a business, a farm or a single investment.

This time, at this hour, I cannot take "No" for an answer. You must cut the capital gains tax on the people of this country. Never has an issue been so demagogued by its opponents. But the demagogues are wrong. They are wrong, and they know it. Sixty percent of people who benefit from lower capital gains have incomes under $50,000. A cut in the capital gains tax increases jobs and helps just about everyone in our country. And so I'm asking you to cut the capital gains tax to a maximum of 15.4%. And I'll tell you, I'll tell you, those of you who say, "Oh no, someone who's comfortable may benefit from this" you kind of remind me of the old definition of the Puritan, who couldn't sleep at night worrying that somehow someone somewhere was out having a good time.

The opponents of this measure and those who've authored various so-called soak-the-rich bills that are floating around this chamber should be reminded of something: When they aim at the big guy, they usually hit the little guy. And maybe it's time that stopped.

This then is my short-term plan. Your part, members of Congress, requires enactment of these common-sense proposals that will have a strong effect on the economy, without breaking the budget agreement and without raising tax rates. And while my plan is being passed and kicking in, we've got to care for those in trouble today. I have provided for up to $4.4 billion in my budget to extend federal unemployment benefits, and I ask for Congressional action right away. And I thank the committee--well, at last. And let's be frank. Let's be frank; let me level with you.

I know, and you know, that my plan is unveiled in a political season. I know, and you know, that everything I propose will be viewed by some in merely partisan terms. But I ask you to know what is in my heart. And my aim is to increase our nation's good. And I'm doing what I think is right; I'm proposing what I know will help. I pride myself that I'm a prudent man, and I believe that patience is a virtue, but I understand politics is, for some, a game and that sometimes the game is to stop all progress and then decry the lack of improvement. But let me tell you, let me tell you, far more important than my political future-- and far more important than yours--is the well-being of our country.

And members of this chamber, members of this chamber, are practical people, and I know you won't resent some practical advice: When people put their party's fortunes, whatever the party, whatever the side of this aisle, before the public good, they court defeat not only for their country, but for themselves. And they will certainly deserve it.

And I submit my plan tomorrow. And I am asking you to pass it by March 20. From the day after that--if it must be--the battle is joined. And you know, when principle is at stake, I relish a good fair fight.

I said my plan has two parts, and it does. And it's the second part that is the heart of the matter. For it's not enough to get an immediate burst. We need long-term improvement in our economic position. We all know that the key to our economic future is to insure that America continues as the economic leader of the world. We have that in our power. Here, then, is my long-term plan to guarantee our future.

First, trade: We will work to break down the walls that stop world trade. We will work to open markets everywhere. And in our major trade negotiations, I will continue pushing to eliminate tariffs and subsidies that damage America's farmers and workers. And we'll get more good American jobs within our own hemisphere through the North American Free Trade Agreement, and through the Enterprise for the Americas Initiative. But changes are here, and more are coming. The work place of the future will demand more highly skilled workers than ever, people who are computer literate, highly educated.

And we must be the world's leader in education. And we must revolutionize America's schools. My America 2000 strategy will help us reach that goal. My plan will give parents more choice, give teachers more flexibility and help communities create new American schools. Thirty states across the nation have established America 2000 programs. Hundreds of cities and towns have joined. Now Congress must join this great movement. Pass my proposals for new American schools.

That was my second long-term proposal. And here's my third: We must make common-sense investments that will help us compete, long-term, in the marketplace. We must encourage research and development. My plan is to make the R and D tax credit permanent, and to provide record levels of support, over $76 billion this year alone for people who explore the promise of emerging technologies.

And fourth, we must do something about crime and drugs. And it is time for a major renewed investment in fighting violent street crime. Its saps our strength and hurts our faith in our society, and in our future together. Surely a tired woman on her way to work at six in the morning on a subway deserves the right to get there safely. And surely, it's true that everyone who changes his or her way of life because of crime--from those afraid to go our at night to those afraid to walk in the parks they pay for--surely those people have been denied a basic civil right. It is time to restore it. Congress, pass my comprehensive crime bill. It is tough on criminals and supportive of police, and it has been languishing in these hallowed halls for years now. Pass it. Help your country.

And fifth, I ask you tonight to fund our HOPE housing proposal and to pass my enterprise-zone legislation, which will get businesses into the inner city. We must empower the poor with the pride that comes from owning a home, getting a job, becoming part of things. My plan would encourage real estate construction by extending tax incentives for mortgage-revenue bonds and low-income housing. And I ask tonight for record expenditures for the program that helps children born into want move into excellence: Head Start.

Step six: We must reform our health care system for this too, bears on whether or not we can compete in the world. American health costs have been exploding. This year America will spend over $800 billion on health, and that is expected to grow to $1.6 trillion by the end of the decade. We simply cannot afford this. The cost of health care shows up not only in your family budget, but in the price of everything we buy and everything we sell. When health coverage for a fellow on the assembly line costs thousands of dollars, the cost goes into the product he makes. And you pay the bill. Now we must make a choice.

Now some pretend we can have it both ways: they call it play or pay. But that expensive approach is unstable. It will mean higher taxes, fewer jobs, and eventually, a system under complete government control. Really, there are only two options. And we can move toward a nationalized system, a system which will restrict patient choice in picking a doctor and force the government to ration services arbitrarily. And what we'll get is patients in long lines, indifferent service and a huge new tax burden. Or we can reform our own private health-care system, which still gives us, for all its flaws, the best quality health care in the world. Well, let's build on our strengths.

My plan provides insurance security for all Americans while preserving and increasing the idea of choice. We make basic health insurance affordable for all low-income people not now covered. We do it by providing a health-insurance tax credit of up to $3750 for each low-income family. The middle class gets help, too. And by reforming the health insurance market, my plan assures that Americans will have access to basic health insurance even if they change jobs or develop serious health problem We must bring costs under control, preserve quality, preserve choice and reduce people's nagging daily worry about health insurance. My plan, the details of which I will announce shortly, does just that.

And seventh, we must get the federal deficit under control. We now have in law, enforcable spending caps, and a requirement that we pay for the programs we create. There are those in Congress who would ease that discipline now. But I cannot let them do it. And I won't. My plan would freeze all domestic discretionary budget authority which means "No more next year than this year". I will not tamper with Social Security but I would put real caps on the growth of uncontrolled spending. And I would also freeze federal domestic government employment. And with the help of Congress, my plan will get rid of 246 programs that don't deserve federal funding. Some of them have noble titles, but none of them is indispensible. We can get rid of each and every one of them.

You know, it's time we rediscovered a home truth the American people have never forgotten: the government is too big and spends too much. And I call on Congress to adopt a measure that will help put an end to the annual ritual of filling the budget with pork-barrel appropriations. Every year, the press has a field day making fun of outrageous examples, a Lawrence Welk Museum, a research grant for Belgian Endive. We all know how these things get into the budget, and maybe you need someone to help you say no. I know how to say it. And you know what I need to make it stick. Give me the same thing 43 governors have--the line-item veto--and let me help you control spending.

We must put an end to unfinanced government mandates. These are the requirements Congress puts on our cities, counties and states without supplying the money. And if Congress passes a mandate, it should be forced to pay for it and balance the cost with savings elsewhere. After all, a mandate just increases someone else's tax burden, and that means higher taxes at the state and local level.

Step Eight: Congress should enact the bold reform proposals that are still awaiting congressional action: bank reform, civil justice reform, tort reform, and my national energy strategy.

And finally, we must strengthen the family, because it is the family that has the greatest bearing on our future. When Barbara holds an AIDS baby in her arms and reads to children, she's saying to every person in this country, "Family Matters".

And I am announcing tonight a new commission on America's urban families. I've asked Missouri's governor, John Ashcroft, to be chairman, former Dallas Mayor Annetter Strauss to be co-chair. You know, I had Mayors, the leading mayors from the League of Cities, in the other day at the White House, and they told me something striking. They said that every one of them, Republican and Democrat, agreed on one thing: That the major cause of the problems of the cities is the dissolution of the family. And they asked for this commission, and they were right to ask, because it's time to determine what we can do to keep families together, strong and sound.

There's one thing we can do right away: Ease the burden of rearing a child. I ask you tonight to raise the personal exemption by $500 per child for every family. For a family with four kids, that's an increase of $2000. This is a good start in the right direction, and it's what we can afford. It's time to allow families to deduct the interest they pay on student loans. And I'm asking you to do just that. And I'm asking you to allow people to use money from their IRAs to pay medical and educational expenses, all without penalties. And I'm asking for more. Ask American parents what they dislike about how things are going in our country, and chances are good that pretty soon they'll get to welfare.

Americans are the most generous people on Earth. But we have to go back to the insight of Franklin Roosevelt who, when he spoke of what became the welfare program, want that it must not become a narcotic and a subtle destroyer of the spirit. Welfare was never meant to be a life style. It was never meant to be a habit. It was never supposed to be passed on from generation to generation like a legacy. It's time to replace the assumptions of the welfare state and help reform the welfare system.

States throughout the country are beginning to operate with new assumptions: that when able-bodied people receive government assistance they have responsibilities to the taxpayer. A responsibility to seek work, education, or job training. A responsibility to get their lives in order. A responsibility to hold their families together and refrain from having children out of wedlock. And a responsibility to obey the law. We are going to help this movement. Often, state reform requires waiving certain federal regulations. I will act to make that process easier and quicker for every state that asks our help. And I want to add, as we make these changes, we work together to improve this system, that our intention is not scapegoating and finger-pointing. If you read the papers or watch TV you know there's been a rise these days in a certain kind of ugliness: racist comments, anti-Semitism, an increased sense of division. Really, this is not us. This is not who we are. And this is not acceptable.

And so you have my plan for America. And I am asking for big things, but I believe in my heart you will do what's right.

And you know, it's kind of an American tradition to show a certain skepticism toward our democratic institutions. I myself have sometimes thought the aging process could be delayed if it had to make its way through Congress. But you will deliberate, and you will discuss, and that is fine. But my friends the people cannot wait. They need help now. And there's a mood among us. People are worried. There has been talk of decline. Someone even said our workers are lazy and uninspired. And I thought, "Really? Go tell Neil Armstrong standing on the moon. Tell the American farmer who feeds his country and the world. Tell the men and women of Desert Storm." Moods come and go, but greatness endures. Our does.

And maybe for a moment it's good to remember what, in the dailyness of our lives, we forget. We are still and ever the freest nation on Earth, the kindest nation on Earth, the strongest nation on Earth. And we have always risen to the occasion. And we are going to lift this nation out of hard times inch by inch and day by day, and those who would stop us better step aside. Because I look at hard times and I make this vow: This will not stand. And so we move on, together, a rising nation, the once and future miracle that is still, this night, the hope of the world.

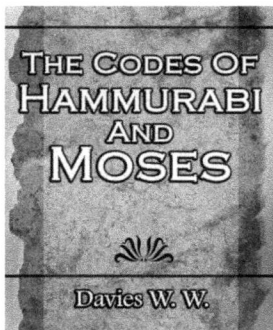

The Codes Of Hammurabi And Moses
W. W. Davies

QTY

The discovery of the Hammurabi Code is one of the greatest achievements of archaeology, and is of paramount interest, not only to the student of the Bible, but also to all those interested in ancient history...

Religion   ISBN: *1-59462-338-4*   **Pages:132**

MSRP $12.95

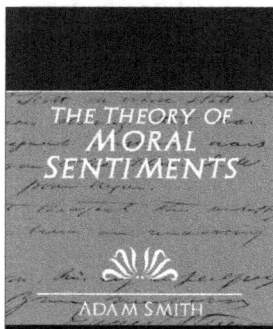

The Theory of Moral Sentiments
Adam Smith

QTY

This work from 1749. contains original theories of conscience amd moral judgment and it is the foundation for systemof morals.

Philosophy ISBN: *1-59462-777-0*   **Pages:536**

MSRP $19.95

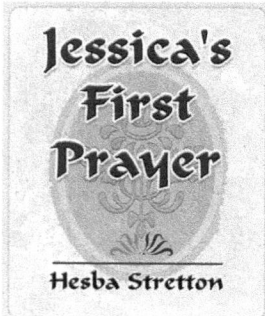

Jessica's First Prayer
Hesba Stretton

QTY

In a screened and secluded corner of one of the many railway-bridges which span the streets of London there could be seen a few years ago, from five o'clock every morning until half past eight, a tidily set-out coffee-stall, consisting of a trestle and board, upon which stood two large tin cans, with a small fire of charcoal burning under each so as to keep the coffee boiling during the early hours of the morning when the work-people were thronging into the city on their way to their daily toil...

Pages:84

Childrens   ISBN: *1-59462-373-2*   *MSRP $9.95*

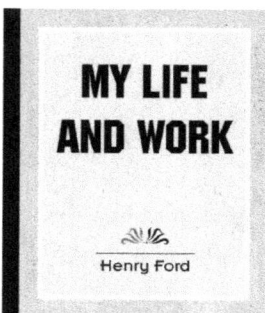

My Life and Work
Henry Ford

QTY

Henry Ford revolutionized the world with his implementation of mass production for the Model T automobile. Gain valuable business insight into his life and work with his own auto-biography... "We have only started on our development of our country we have not as yet, with all our talk of wonderful progress, done more than scratch the surface. The progress has been wonderful enough but..."

Pages:300

Biographies/   ISBN: *1-59462-198-5*   *MSRP $21.95*

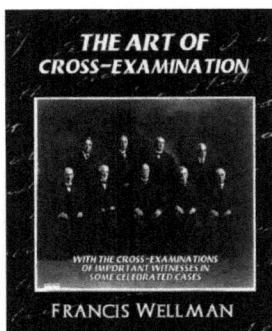

The Art of Cross-Examination
Francis Wellman

QTY

I presume it is the experience of every author, after his first book is published upon an important subject, to be almost overwhelmed with a wealth of ideas and illustrations which could readily have been included in his book, and which to his own mind, at least, seem to make a second edition inevitable. Such certainly was the case with me; and when the first edition had reached its sixth impression in five months, I rejoiced to learn that it seemed to my publishers that the book had met with a sufficiently favorable reception to justify a second and considerably enlarged edition. ..

Pages:412

Reference   **ISBN: *1-59462-647-2***   *MSRP $19.95*

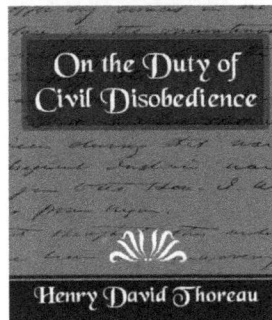

On the Duty of Civil Disobedience
Henry David Thoreau

QTY

Thoreau wrote his famous essay, On the Duty of Civil Disobedience, as a protest against an unjust but popular war and the immoral but popular institution of slave-owning. He did more than write—he declined to pay his taxes, and was hauled off to gaol in consequence. Who can say how much this refusal of his hastened the end of the war and of slavery ?

Law   **ISBN: *1-59462-747-9***   **Pages:48**

MSRP $7.45

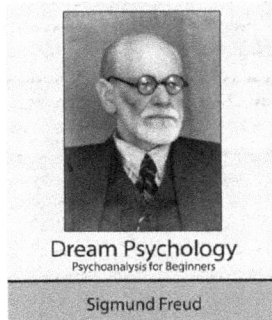

Dream Psychology Psychoanalysis for Beginners
Sigmund Freud

QTY

Sigmund Freud, born Sigismund Schlomo Freud (May 6, 1856 - September 23, 1939), was a Jewish-Austrian neurologist and psychiatrist who co-founded the psychoanalytic school of psychology. Freud is best known for his theories of the unconscious mind, especially involving the mechanism of repression; his redefinition of sexual desire as mobile and directed towards a wide variety of objects; and his therapeutic techniques, especially his understanding of transference in the therapeutic relationship and the presumed value of dreams as sources of insight into unconscious desires.

Pages:196

Psychology   **ISBN: *1-59462-905-6***   *MSRP $15.45*

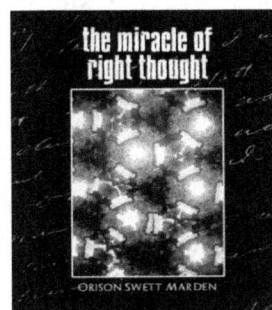

The Miracle of Right Thought
Orison Swett Marden

QTY

Believe with all of your heart that you will do what you were made to do. When the mind has once formed the habit of holding cheerful, happy, prosperous pictures, it will not be easy to form the opposite habit. It does not matter how improbable or how far away this realization may see, or how dark the prospects may be, if we visualize them as best we can, as vividly as possible, hold tenaciously to them and vigorously struggle to attain them, they will gradually become actualized, realized in the life. But a desire, a longing without endeavor, a yearning abandoned or held indifferently will vanish without realization.

Pages:360

Self Help   **ISBN: *1-59462-644-8***   *MSRP $25.45*

QTY

☐ **The Rosicrucian Cosmo-Conception Mystic Christianity** by *Max Heindel* ISBN: 1-59462-188-8 **$38.95**
The Rosicrucian Cosmo-conception is not dogmatic, neither does it appeal to any other authority than the reason of the student. It is: not controversial, but is: sent forth in the, hope that it may help to clear... New Age/Religion Pages 646

☐ **Abandonment To Divine Providence** by *Jean-Pierre de Caussade* ISBN: 1-59462-228-0 **$25.95**
"The Rev. Jean Pierre de Caussade was one of the most remarkable spiritual writers of the Society of Jesus in France in the 18th Century. His death took place at Toulouse in 1751. His works have gone through many editions and have been republished... Inspirational/Religion Pages 400

☐ **Mental Chemistry** by *Charles Haanel* ISBN: 1-59462-192-6 **$23.95**
Mental Chemistry allows the change of material conditions by combining and appropriately utilizing the power of the mind. Much like applied chemistry creates something new and unique out of careful combinations of chemicals the mastery of mental chemistry... New Age Pages 354

☐ **The Letters of Robert Browning and Elizabeth Barret Barrett 1845-1846 vol II** ISBN: 1-59462-193-4 **$35.95**
by *Robert Browning* and *Elizabeth Barrett* Biographies Pages 596

☐ **Gleanings In Genesis (volume I)** by *Arthur W. Pink* ISBN: 1-59462-130-6 **$27.45**
Appropriately has Genesis been termed "the seed plot of the Bible" for in it we have, in germ form, almost all of the great doctrines which are afterwards fully developed in the books of Scripture which follow... Religion/Inspirational Pages 420

☐ **The Master Key** by *L. W. de Laurence* ISBN: 1-59462-001-6 **$30.95**
In no branch of human knowledge has there been a more lively increase of the spirit of research during the past few years than in the study of Psychology, Concentration and Mental Discipline. The requests for authentic lessons in Thought Control, Mental Discipline and... New Age/Business Pages 422

☐ **The Lesser Key Of Solomon Goetia** by *L. W. de Laurence* ISBN: 1-59462-092-X **$9.95**
This translation of the first book of the "Lernegton" which is now for the first time made accessible to students of Talismanic Magic was done, after careful collation and edition, from numerous Ancient Manuscripts in Hebrew, Latin, and French... New Age/Occult Pages 92

☐ **Rubaiyat Of Omar Khayyam** by *Edward Fitzgerald* ISBN:1-59462-332-5 **$13.95**
Edward Fitzgerald, whom the world has already learned, in spite of his own efforts to remain within the shadow of anonymity, to look upon as one of the rarest poets of the century, was born at Bredfield, in Suffolk, on the 31st of March, 1809. He was the third son of John Purcell... Music Pages 172

☐ **Ancient Law** by *Henry Maine* ISBN: 1-59462-128-4 **$29.95**
The chief object of the following pages is to indicate some of the earliest ideas of mankind, as they are reflected in Ancient Law, and to point out the relation of those ideas to modern thought. Religion/History Pages 452

☐ **Far-Away Stories** by *William J. Locke* ISBN: 1-59462-129-2 **$19.45**
"Good wine needs no bush, but a collection of mixed vintages does. And this book is just such a collection. Some of the stories I do not want to remain buried for ever in the museum files of dead magazine-numbers an author's not unpardonable vanity..." Fiction Pages 272

☐ **Life of David Crockett** by *David Crockett* ISBN: 1-59462-250-7 **$27.45**
"Colonel David Crockett was one of the most remarkable men of the times in which he lived. Born in humble life, but gifted with a strong will, an indomitable courage, and unremitting perseverance... Biographies/New Age Pages 424

☐ **Lip-Reading** by *Edward Nitchie* ISBN: 1-59462-206-X **$25.95**
Edward B. Nitchie, founder of the New York School for the Hard of Hearing, now the Nitchie School of Lip-Reading, Inc, wrote "LIP-READING Principles and Practice". The development and perfecting of this meritorious work on lip-reading was an undertaking... How-to Pages 400

☐ **A Handbook of Suggestive Therapeutics, Applied Hypnotism, Psychic Science** ISBN: 1-59462-214-0 **$24.95**
by *Henry Munro* Health/New Age/Health/Self-help Pages 376

☐ **A Doll's House: and Two Other Plays** by *Henrik Ibsen* ISBN: 1-59462-112-8 **$19.95**
Henrik Ibsen created this classic when in revolutionary 1848 Rome. Introducing some striking concepts in playwriting for the realist genre, this play has been studied the world over. Fiction/Classics/Plays 308

☐ **The Light of Asia** by *sir Edwin Arnold* ISBN: 1-59462-204-3 **$13.95**
In this poetic masterpiece, Edwin Arnold describes the life and teachings of Buddha. The man who was to become known as Buddha to the world was born as Prince Gautama of India but he rejected the worldly riches and abandoned the reigns of power when... Religion/History/Biographies Pages 170

☐ **The Complete Works of Guy de Maupassant** by *Guy de Maupassant* ISBN: 1-59462-157-8 **$16.95**
"For days and days, nights and nights, I had dreamed of that first kiss which was to consecrate our engagement, and I knew not on what spot I should put my lips..." Fiction/Classics Pages 240

☐ **The Art of Cross-Examination** by *Francis L. Wellman* ISBN: 1-59462-309-0 **$26.95**
Written by a renowned trial lawyer, Wellman imparts his experience and uses case studies to explain how to use psychology to extract desired information through questioning. How-to/Science/Reference Pages 408

☐ **Answered or Unanswered?** by *Louisa Vaughan* ISBN: 1-59462-248-5 **$10.95**
Miracles of Faith in China Religion Pages 112

☐ **The Edinburgh Lectures on Mental Science (1909)** by *Thomas* ISBN: 1-59462-008-3 **$11.95**
This book contains the substance of a course of lectures recently given by the writer in the Queen Street Hall, Edinburgh. Its purpose is to indicate the Natural Principles governing the relation between Mental Action and Material Conditions... New Age/Psychology Pages 148

☐ **Ayesha** by *H. Rider Haggard* ISBN: 1-59462-301-5 **$24.95**
Verily and indeed it is the unexpected that happens! Probably if there was one person upon the earth from whom the Editor of this, and of a certain previous history, did not expect to hear again... Classics Pages 380

☐ **Ayala's Angel** by *Anthony Trollope* ISBN: 1-59462-352-X **$29.95**
The two girls were both pretty, but Lucy who was twenty-one who supposed to be simple and comparatively unattractive, whereas Ayala was credited, as her Bombwhat romantic name might show, with poetic charm and a taste for romance. Ayala when her father died was nineteen... Fiction Pages 484

☐ **The American Commonwealth** by *James Bryce* ISBN: 1-59462-286-8 **$34.45**
An interpretation of American democratic political theory. It examines political mechanics and society from the perspective of Scotsman James Bryce Politics Pages 572

☐ **Stories of the Pilgrims** by *Margaret P. Pumphrey* ISBN: 1-59462-116-0 **$17.95**
This book explores pilgrims religious oppression in England as well as their escape to Holland and eventual crossing to America on the Mayflower, and their early days in New England... History Pages 268

QTY

The Fasting Cure *by Sinclair Upton*   ISBN: *1-59462-222-1* $13.95

In the Cosmopolitan Magazine for May, 1910, and in the Contemporary Review (London) for April, 1910, I published an article dealing with my experiences in fasting. I have written a great many magazine articles, but never one which attracted so much attention...   New Age/Self Help/Health Pages 164

Hebrew Astrology *by Sepharial*   ISBN: *1-59462-308-2* $13.45

In these days of advanced thinking it is a matter of common observation that we have left many of the old landmarks behind and that we are now pressing forward to greater heights and to a wider horizon than that which represented the mind-content of our progenitors...   Astrology Pages 144

Thought Vibration or The Law of Attraction in the Thought World   ISBN: *1-59462-127-6* $12.95

by William Walker Atkinson   Psychology/Religion Pages 144

Optimism *by Helen Keller*   ISBN: *1-59462-108-X* $15.95

Helen Keller was blind, deaf, and mute since 19 months old, yet famously learned how to overcome these handicaps, communicate with the world, and spread her lectures promoting optimism. An inspiring read for everyone...   Biographies/Inspirational Pages 84

Sara Crewe *by Frances Burnett*   ISBN: *1-59462-360-0* $9.45

In the first place, Miss Minchin lived in London. Her home was a large, dull, tall one, in a large, dull square, where all the houses were alike, and all the sparrows were alike, and where all the door-knockers made the same heavy sound...   Childrens/Classic Pages 88

The Autobiography of Benjamin Franklin *by Benjamin Franklin*   ISBN: *1-59462-135-7* $24.95

The Autobiography of Benjamin Franklin has probably been more extensively read than any other American historical work, and no other book of its kind has had such ups and downs of fortune. Franklin lived for many years in England, where he was agent...   Biographies/History Pages 332

Name	
Email	
Telephone	
Address	
City, State ZIP	

☐ **Credit Card**   ☐ **Check / Money Order**

Credit Card Number	
Expiration Date	
Signature	

Please Mail to: Book Jungle
PO Box 2226
Champaign, IL 61825
or Fax to: 630-214-0564

ORDERING INFORMATION

web: *www.bookjungle.com*
email: *sales@bookjungle.com*
fax: *630-214-0564*
mail: *Book Jungle PO Box 2226 Champaign, IL 61825*
or PayPal *to sales@bookjungle.com*

Please contact us for bulk discounts

DIRECT-ORDER TERMS

**20% Discount if You Order
Two or More Books**
Free Domestic Shipping!
Accepted: Master Card, Visa,
Discover, American Express